THE
Archive Photographs
SERIES

CHELMSFORD

Detail from photograph on page 24 showing workers from Hoffman's and Marconi's going home after a day's work in 1957.

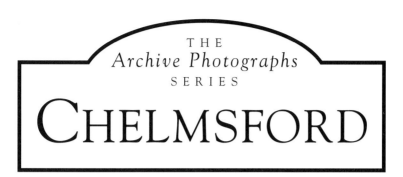

THE
Archive Photographs
SERIES

CHELMSFORD

Compiled by
Stan Jarvis

CHALFORD

First published 1997
Copyright © Stan Jarvis, 1997

The Chalford Publishing Company
St Mary's Mill, Chalford,
Stroud, Gloucestershire, GL6 8NX

ISBN 0 7524 0734 1

Typesetting and origination by
The Chalford Publishing Company
Printed in Great Britain by
Redwood Books, Trowbridge

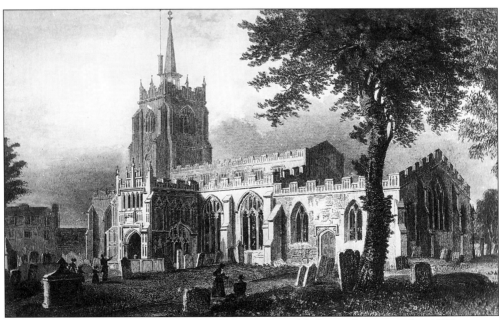

St Mary's, the parish church, before the clerestory was added over the east end in 1878.

Contents

Acknowledgements

My good friend Peter Russell,
Louisa Stringer, Local Studies Librarian
and her colleagues
at Chelmsford Central Library

Introduction

Chelmsford started as a Roman camp – an overnight stop on the way from the Thames, through the Forest of Essex to the invaders' target, the great British settlement at Colchester. In their subsequent journeyings this halfway house gave Chelmsford significance as a market centre where Romans and natives could meet for peaceful trading. Even though Colchester was of far greater importance, it was Chelmsford's favourable situation in the centre of the county as it developed, and its closeness to the seat of national government in London which achieved it the status of 'County Town' with the offices and courts and business it involved.

Through the years the simple settlement expanded to Elizabethan, then Georgian grandeur, from Bishop's Hall and Moulsham Hall to the Shire Hall and the Stone Bridge. An important market was held in Tindal Square and its associated streets right through to Victorian times, bringing people in from a wide rural area to do their shopping in all the exciting bustle.

From the end of the nineteenth century, now fully accepted as the County town, Chelmsford drew businessmen looking for suitable sites for factories and workshops. Their workers needed homes, so building became another important local industry. People were drawn to the new industries from all over Essex and beyond, and more and more of Chelmsford's rural area was developed. New traders, department stores and businesses moved into the High Street and prospered from the custom of the new residents.

The art of photography, developed from about 1840, became the most popular of the visual arts invented and one family, the Spaldings, were there to answer the local demand and reap the benefit. Frederick Spalding came to Chelmsford in the middle of the nineteenth century when he set up in business as a 'bird stuffer and furniture broker' – to quote the *Essex County Directory* of 1859. He was a child of the Industrial Revolution whose imagination was captured by photography. He bought the necessary, bulky equipment and the chemicals and by the next directory, in 1862, his business was revised as 'Picture-frame maker and photographer'. He was the only 'Photographic Artist' in the town at that time, so it is not surprising that his business flourished and prospered. His first child, Frederick, who was born in 1858, followed in his footsteps. He went to Chelmsford Grammar School when it was in Duke Street and saw the swirl of the town's life every day as he passed through the High Street and Tindal Square. He took over the business and photographed people from every walk of life – from the Prince of Wales with the Countess of Warwick at Easton Lodge, to Dick the Pieman straight off his pitch in Chelmsford market. But more than that, he photographed buildings of all kinds, old and new, which graced his home town. His own son, Frederick, the third, came back from the war as a pilot to take, in 1920, the first ever aerial view of the town.

The glass plates, and later the negatives and prints, piled up in the shop; many fully documented, others not so. He died in 1947 after a distinguished life in local government: a member of the town council for fifty-four years and three times Mayor. The late F.G. Emmison, County Archivist, often told the story of how the surviving Spalding photographs came to the Record Office: '... in 1954 I received a phone call: "Your name has been given to me as a man keen on old things ... we're clearing out a shop in the High Street with a big lot of old photos. If you're interested could you collect 'em pretty quickly, or they'll all go ... The office porter and I brought away a mass of postcards and prints, when I was shown a further mass – of glass negatives ..."'

I myself had the pleasure, as Deputy Borough Librarian and Museum Curator, of going to a garage of a house and collecting a number of Fred Spalding's own annotated albums of original photographs which were literally awaiting the dustman's visit! These two collections are now united in the Essex Record Office, though it must be said that the Chelmsford Library still preserves many other 'Spaldings' collected over the years from a variety of sources.

Other photographs in this book, by skilled photographers like Peter Russell, have been included to give comparisons with Spalding's day. The life of Chelmsford since it became a Borough in 1888 is pictured here to the extent of my own collection, which has been assembled over many years. Should your imagination be fired to further research you will be sure of a welcome at the Essex Record Office and at the Chelmsford Library where the full range of photographs and postcards of the County Town can be enjoyed.

One

A Walk
Through History

The third generation of Fred Spaldings, an air force pilot, flew over his home town to take this view in 1920. From the left Duke Street runs into Tindal Square from where New Street runs off to the right.

A model based on the excavated remains of a Roman building believed to be a stopping place for messengers on imperial business from London to Colchester.

Proof of Roman occupation, a bronze statuette of a cockerel, one of the creatures associated with the Roman god Mercury, found on the site of the 'mansio', built in the first century A.D.

A copy of an eighteenth-century print showing the parish church, now the Cathedral, and the Shire Hall shortly after its erection in 1791.

A view down Duke Street in 1870 showing the railway bridge, here about twenty-five years old, and the tower and spire of St Mary's church, now the Cathedral, rising above it.

OLD HOUSES. Duke Street Chelmsford Previously Known as Kings St

Fair Field was also
The Cricket Field

W. G. Grace played
on this ground —

Entrance
to
Fair Field

Mrs Rolfe
Marine Store

Mr Warner
Wood
Turner

Mr Wilkinson
Sweep

Mr Shead
Baker

Mr Hay
Boot m

Demolished 1875   Now the site of The War Memorial and Rainsford Ho

Old houses in Duke Street as seen in 1875 by an unknown artist, just before their demolition, copied by Fred Spalding and with his added comments, such as he gave on many of the photographs. The Chelmsford Civic Centre and the War Memorial now stand here.

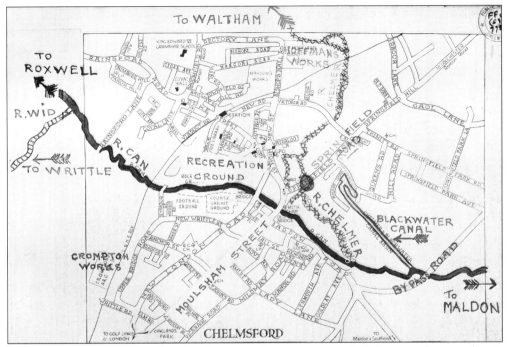

Spalding's map helps to identify places in the previous and following photographs. It emphasises the two rivers, the Chelmer and the Can, and the headwaters of the Chelmer and Blackwater Canal.

A wider view by the same pilot of Chelmsford in 1920. Spalding's photographic studio and gift shop is in the dead centre, the third shop to the left of the Shire Hall.

13

Compare the previous view with this aerial photograph of 1985.

The first big house in town, approaching from the west, was Rainsford House, on the left. It was demolished in 1961 when the purpose-built Civic Centre took its place. This is how it looked in 1928. Further down on the left the County Hotel is still evident.

The house at the junction of Duke Street and Fairfield Road is about to be demolished to make room for the extension of the bus station. Called Fairfield House, it had been lived in by Dr Henry Newton. By 1932 it was a pile of rubble.

People had to be asked to stand still while the plate in the camera was exposed, a hundred years ago. The sight of the parish church, now the Cathedral, down the path on the extreme right makes this location easily recognized.

Here we have arrived at Tindal Square where the good judge Tindal, seated on a stone plinth, broods over a quiet morning one day at the end of the nineteenth century. Spalding's shop is second from the right.

16

Tindal Square in 1926. The statue has now been re-aligned, but all the buildings carry on the same businesses today.

The Shire Hall from the neck of the High Street in 1978. The High Street is now pedestrianised.

Two originals for Spalding postcards sold in the shop which is shown in the lower photograph, taken at the turn of the century. The comments in Spalding's hand are typical of his interest in the town of which he became mayor.

The obverse and reverse of a copper halfpenny token issued in 1794 by Thomas Clachar, owner of the Chelmsford Chronicle, to pay his workers when coins of the realm were in short supply. He took the Shire Hall as his emblem of good faith and honesty.

Tindal Square around 1880. The blur in the road by the lamppost marks the passage of a penny farthing cyclist whilst the plate was exposed.

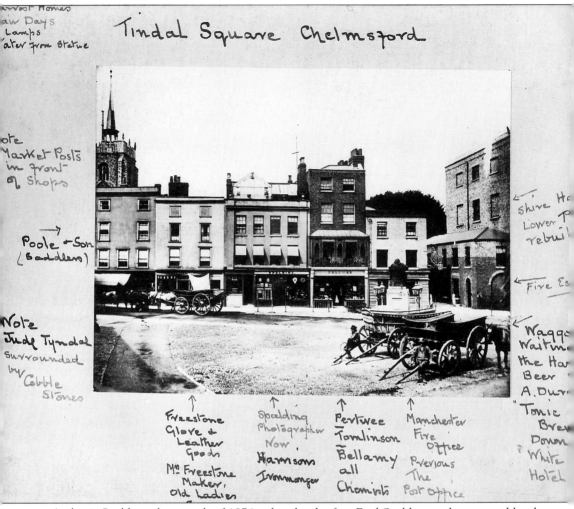

A classic Spalding photograph of 1874, taken by the first Fred Spalding and annotated by the second for his album.

In 1880 Fred Spalding tried his hand at painting the view from his shop, including the houses down the High Street on the left and Catt's the grocers on the right.

A print prepared by Spalding for one of his lectures which shows Tindal Square in 1831, with a coach heading up Duke Street to the Epping road.

A painting by W. Brown dated 1882, of the upper High Street. Shops on the left include Smith's the drapers, Durrant's the booksellers, Bush the chemists and, on the far corner, the Manchester Fire Office, formerly the Post Office.

An undated picture but the horse-droppings in the foreground show that it predates the internal combustion engine and is later than 1907, the year that Shire Hall got its clock.

A postcard of the same scene, *c.* 1910.

Behind the Shire Hall and the Cathedral lies Cottage Place, shown here as it was in the early years of Victoria's reign.

This view takes us a little further down New Street, dated for us in the familiar handwriting of Fred Spalding.

Further along again, and much later, in 1957, we see workers from Hoffman's and Marconi's going home after a day's work. The two factories can be discerned on either side of the railway arch which has been rebuilt since then.

A diversion to Central Park to see the wreckage of a huge, old willow, blown down in the gale of March, 1986.

Back in the High Street in 1880. Blurs on the print are caused by movement in the view during exposure of the plate in the camera. The posts on the right hand side had a rope drawn through them on market days to make a hitching rail for farmers' horses.

Two of the first houses in the High Street. Number 2 is decorated for the accession of Edward VII in 1901, by its owner, Frederick Chancellor. They were replaced by Barclay's Bank. Frederick Chancellor was the first Mayor of Chelmsford. Appointed in 1888, he served six more times in that capacity before his death in 1918, aged ninety-two.

Number 4, High Street as it looked in 1880 when John Champ lived there. Fred Spalding took it over for his shop and was still in business there in the 1950s. A postscript – Fred Spalding died in 1947. His shop was closed and hundreds of his plates, slides and prints lay scattered about in the shop until 1954 when the late Dr F. Emmison was able, personally, to collect them and take them for recording and safe-keeping in the Essex Record Office of which he was County Archivist.

A rare photograph from around 1870 taken by the first Fred Spalding. The 'Conduit' has been moved here from Tindal Square to make room for the Tindal statue.

Fred Spalding, junior, took a very similar view some forty years later, to show how many more houses had been converted to shops.

A sketch by an unknown artist from the eighteenth century, who had turned down Springfield Road at the bottom of the town to show us what Chelmsford looked like from Springfield meadows, some two hundred years ago.

This view of Springfield watermill, The Shire Hall and the church of St Mary was drawn by J. Greig for tourists taking *Excursions through Essex* in 1819.

The High Street/Springfield Road junction in 1962. Nearly every shop in view has since changed hands.

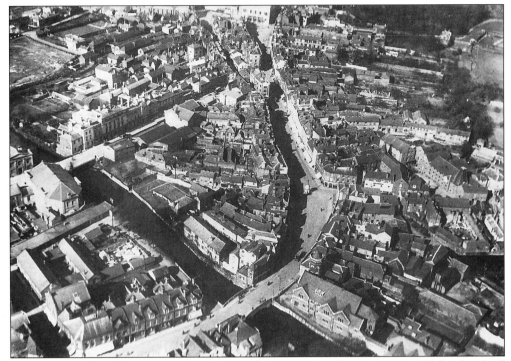

A last look at the town centre, the first aerial photograph of it, taken in 1920 by the third generation of Spalding photographers.

The celebrated Stone Bridge as it looked in 1900. The date of its erection, 1787, is clearly shown on the keystone.

The Stone Bridge, or Bishop's Bridge over the River Can, built in 1787, seen here in 1890.

The new 'Iron Bridge' over the Can replaced the one washed away in the great flood of 1888 and was opened 1 November 1890.

An old postcard introduces us to Moulsham, the former hamlet, where the road leads on from the Stone Bridge, *c.* 1907.

Moulsham Street in the sunshine some ninety years ago with the Baddow Road turning on the left. All the road up to that point has now been pedestrianised.

Another view of Moulsham Street, nearer the Baddow Road corner. On the extreme right is the Co-operative grocery shop built on the site of the old gaol in 1880. This photograph was taken before 1896.

Another old Moulsham building in process of demolition, numbers 28 and 29, in 1931. The octagonal tower of the Methodist church down by the Stone Bridge gives us our bearings.

These old houses on the corner of Moulsham Street and The Friars were all in a sorry state when photographed in the 'thirties, but they and their successors were all cleared away when Parkway, the inner relief road was under construction in 1962.

Two

Events

This print of 1762 depicts the ancient custom of marking the opening of the Court of Assize in the County Town. The judge makes a grand entrance in a carriage headed by a column of pikemen, to guarantee his safety, and a mounted escort of county officers and buglers seen here beneath the sign of the old Lion inn.

Market Day in the High Street, drawn by Mrs Susanne Alston prior to the disastrous fire of 1805. The view is from the bottom of the High Street, with Springfield Road running from the righthand corner.

High Street Chelmsford July 19ᵗ 1821
Celebration of the Coronation of His Majesty George 4ᵗʰ

ry Frances Hamilton delt.

HIGH STREET, CHELMSFORD,
as it appeared on the 19ᵗʰ July 1821 at the Celebration of the Coronation of his
MAJESTY KING GEORGE THE FOURTH.

The gentry of Chelmsford opened a subscription to provide a dinner for 1,500 poor people in celebration of George IV's coronation in 1820. A pamphlet was published telling the whole story. It can still be read in the Chelmsford Library.

Chelmsford was honoured as the County town chosen for the Royal Agricultural Society's Exhibition of 1856 to be held on the old sports field, off New Street in the shadow of the railway embankment. The trains began running in Chelmsford from 1845.

The West Essex Militia Band at practice on the old Barrack Square in about 1870. They include Bandmaster Charles Byford, Drum Major W. Byford, H. Byford, three Fletchers, two Barkers and a Drake, none of whom can now be personally identified.

Penny farthings seen in the museum look perilous things, but here is proof of their popularity when, in 1883, the cycling clubs of Essex met at Chelmsford. Robert Cook, in the foreground, was secretary of the Chelmsford club.

Fred Spalding was on hand to record the Great Flood and the effects it had on the town, on 2 August 1888, as efficiently as any modern news reporter.

Further along London Road.

The Stone Bridge held but the BaddowRoad was submerged.

In the High Street crowds of people enjoyed the novelty of paddling round the shops.

The Moulsham side of the Stone Bridge. The coat of arms, or badge, on the second building from the right indicates that this is the former House of Correction.

Another crowd of excited children, and not a few adults, gathers at the approach to the Stone Bridge in the High Street.

From a risky perch on the Stone Bridge Fred Spalding recorded the surge of the swollen river.

The effects of the flood were even felt in Springfield Road where less daring folk were taken about their business by horse and cart.

Our last view of the Great Flood of 1888 is by the remains of the Iron Bridge in London Road, which was smashed and washed away by the strength of the current. The policeman stands river-side of the rough barricade.

Reading the Charter by Mr A.J. Furbank Sep 19th 1888
Mr Frank Whitmore acted as Mayor from the date of the Charter until [

Chelmsford, County Town from ancient times, did not receive its Charter of Incorporation as a Borough until 19 September 1888. Spalding photographed the historic scene as the Charter, brought by train from London, was read out to a huge crowd outside the Corn Exchange.

When the railway ferry SS *Chelmsford* was launched at Hull in 1893 the owners, the Great Eastern Railway, invited all the Chelmsford Councillors to attend and celebrate the occasion. What fun they had! Among them was Councillor Fred Spalding, the furthermost man on the left of the top picture. Note the bow of the ship above, and the broken bottle in the picture below.

Everybody knows the Saracen's Head, seen here in the 1890s when the Chelmsford Cycling Club showed off the best in British cycles – the 'tall ordinaries' or penny farthings.

A group of eminent Essex personalities including mayors and their footmen (one at each end) at the great athletic event of the year – the Essex County Athletic Race Meeting of 10 July 1897.

The reason for this great gathering outside the Shire Hall , even after much research, seems to be lost forever. It is possible that it shows the announcement of the results of an election, eagerly awaited by the crowd.

A young officer stands stiffly to attention after being presented to his hero, the great Lord Roberts of Kandahar. The formal opening of the Territorial Army Drill Hall (demolished in 1996) is over, and all county and military society is to be seen at the subsequent garden party.

The tea party held in the new Drill Hall on 4 July 1903 after its opening by Lord Roberts.

On 28 January 1911 the Essex Union Hunt brought their foxhounds to a meet in Tindal Square as a reminder of the old days when Chelmsford was the centre of country life for miles around. They gathered in the view of a great crowd outside the Shire Hall. New Street is to the right.

On 27 June 1912 Claude Graham-White married Dorothy Taylor of New York at Widford church and they had their reception at Hylands, now owned by the Borough. He was the first Englishman to get his pilot's licence.

The Essex Hunt had 'carted' a deer as a live quarry for the hounds on a winter's day in the 1930s. It took to the river in the Recreation Ground, was captured and released back to its woodland habitat. The railway viaduct can just be discerned behind the trees.

Eight silver drums being presented to the 'Pompadours', the Essex Regiment, in 1913. They were bought for them by the people of Essex.

In 1926 the public responded again to an appeal for money to provide an extra six drums for the 1st Battalion, the Essex Regiment.

The first house in Chelmsford to be damaged by a bomb. It was dropped from a Zeppelin in the night of 24 September 1916 onto a cottage in Becket's Row, Glebe Road. Although the inhabitants were very shocked there were no injuries.

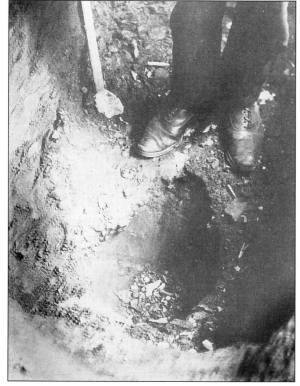

The crater made by the bomb under the cottage floor – and the feet of the special constable sent to guard it until it could be properly investigated.

An aerial view of the Chelmsford racecourse on Galleywood Common in about 1930. By 1935 it had been reduced to pony racing, which was finished for good with the advent of the Second World War.

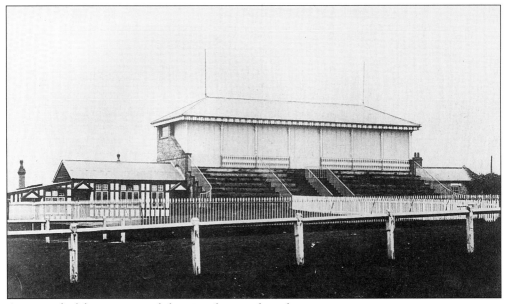

A postcard of the same period showing the grandstand.

A photographer for the *Essex Chronicle* recorded the Chelmsford Racecourse on Galleywood Common in March 1939 when it was offered for sale by auction.

It is May 25 1932, and HRH Prince George has come to the town to declare open Chelmsford's first bypass, running from Widford to Springfield in a wide curve round what was then the edge of the town.

The Prince went on to the museum at Oaklands where he paused to receive three cheers from an enthusiastic crowd.

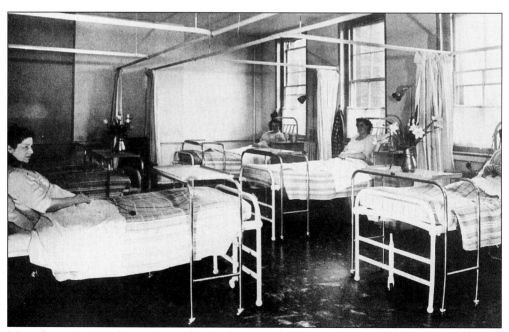

More 'happy events' have occurred here than anywhere else in town! The maternity ward at St John's Hospital in 1955.

Three
Public Service

Chelmsford, or King Edward VI, Grammar School, when it was rebuilt and refounded in 1551, stood in Duke Street on a site now covered by County Hall. By 1890 four classes were being conducted in its hall. Judge Tindal (1776-1846) was one of its famous scholars.

Frank W. Rogers, Headmaster, poses with staff and scholars outside the Grammar School in 1890-1 when there were 150 pupils.

The old Grammar School awaiting demolition in 1932. The new school in Broomfield Road was open in 1892.

Shire Hall Chelmsford Erected 1791 By John Johnson architect
The 3 grouped figures under the pediment represent
Justice — Wisdom — Mercy

Chaise Note Milkman Note No Cannon Th old Saracen

In the Lower portion the Corn-market was formerly held. Auctioneers sold just outside the Building

The earliest-known print of the Shire Hall with marginal notes by Fred Spalding.

Proof of Chelmsford's importance as a county centre is provided by this print of the Polytechnic Exhibition held there in 1848 and specially drawn for publication by Frederick Chancellor, a well-known Essex architect who lived in the town.

The Shire Hall after 1907, when the clock was placed on it and before the onset of motor traffic. 'Spalding, Photographer' can be read on the facade of the shop on the extreme right.

In 1936, knowing that the Shire Hall was about to undergo considerable interior reconstruction, Fred Spalding popped in with his camera to record for posterity just what the old place had looked like in his younger days. The work was carried out by local builder A.J. Arnold at a cost of £16,695. Here we see the vestibule.

The Crown Court, Shire Hall, in 1936.

The Nisi Prius Court, Shire Hall, in 1936.

Some sixty years later, in 1969, we can see some of the traffic congestion which beset the High Street until pedestrianisation a few years ago.

Fred Spalding copied an old print of Chelmsford's first gas supply in 1819 on a site down by the canal.

The Corn Exchange in Tindal Square was opened just a year before Fred Spalding's birth in 1858. He photographed this print and tells us that the design was by Frederick Chancellor who went on to become Chelmsford's first mayor. He is remembered in the name of the modern building on the site – the Chancellor Hall.

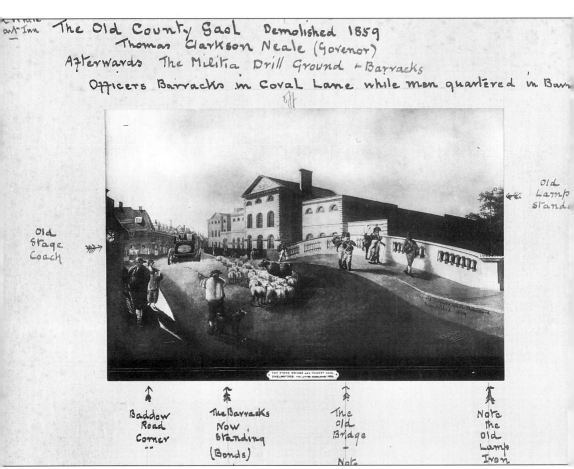

The Old County Gaol   Demolished 1859
Thomas Clarkson Neale (Governor)
Afterwards The Militia Drill Ground + Barracks
Officers Barracks in Coval Lane while men quartered in Barr

Old Lamp Stand

Old Stage Coach

Baddow Road Corner
--

The Barracks Now Standing (Bonds)

The old Bridge
Note

Note the old Lamp Iron

Spalding's own copy print of the old County Gaol carries some helpful inscriptions. It had been rebuilt in 1777 and the House of Correction beyond it was put up in 1806.

The same photographer was called in to make a photographic record of the present prison built on Springfield Hill in 1828 after it had been functioning for a century. He started at the entrance...

...went under the arch to the inner courtyard...

...and on to the...

...warders' desk and then to...

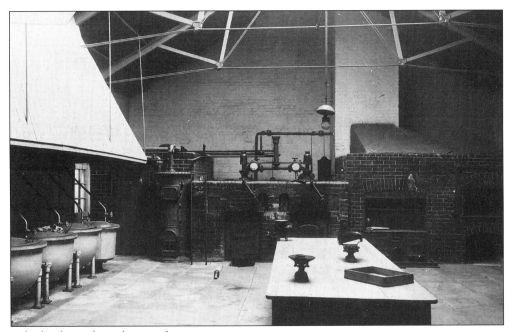

...the kitchen, along the corridor...

...and finally up the metal stairway to...

...rows of cells on the ground floor. A severe fire about twenty years ago and a more modern approach to ideas of punishment have resulted in various alterations since this time.

Back in the centre of the town we see County Hall photographed from the other side of Duke Street and just after its completion to the design of R. Stuart in 1935.

After fifty years it needed an extension and is seen here at its opening by Her Majesty the Queen in 1988 to applause led by her Lord Lieutenant for Essex, Admiral Sir Andrew Lewis.

A general view of the offices included in the new extension.

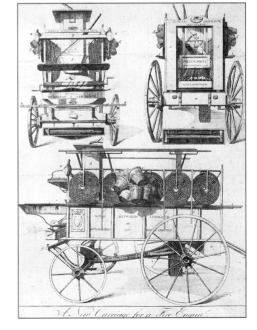

William Stanes, agent for Royal Exchange Assurance, brought out this new design for a horse-drawn fire engine in 1775 or thereabouts. He was also a Chelmsford schoolmaster and bookseller.

The Chelmsford Fire Brigade has a special turn-out on Mayor's Day, 1888, when the town first received its charter as a Borough.

The Brigade, much reinforced, parade once again, in 1912, outside the Fire Station which was then in Market Road. The shafts and the whips are visible but the horses have been left in the stables!

This figure, now to be seen in the Shire Hall, once graced the fountainhead where the Tindal statue was later placed. According to Wright's *History of Essex*, 1834, 'Near the Shire Hall there is a conduit supplied with a copious ever running stream from a spring, named Burgess' Well, a short distance from the town. Formerly there was an elegant figure or naiad on the top, which is now occupied by the gaslight lamp; and lower down there were the arms Mainchart, Duke of Schomberg and Earl of Fitzwalter.'

Fred Spalding went to the garden of Springfield Villa to record the last resting place of the naiad and her pedestal. Sometime around 1950 she was rediscovered and returned to the town's rightful keeping. Unfortunately she was considered too frail to be subjected any longer to the open air and was finally found a home in the Shire Hall.

Conduit, Re-built by the Parish, 1852.

We are grateful to Fred Spalding for the further history of the 'Conduit' as shown in these four photographs.

The Tindal statue on the conduit's original site. The inscription reads: 'Erected A.D. 1850. To preserve for all time the image of a Judge, whose administration of English Law – directed by serene wisdom – animated by purest love of justice – endeared by unwearied kindness and graced by the most lucid style will be held by his country in undying remembrance.'

The Conduit being prepared for its removal and relocation in Tower Gardens in 1940.

The Conduit re-erected in Tower Gardens in 1940 where it still makes a charming centrepiece.

This view of Sandford Mill, formerly a water-driven flour mill, was taken in 1929 upon completion of the new waterworks alongside it.

Mr Spalding was commissioned to take further photographs of the new waterworks.

Railway Station, Chelmsford.

The railway station in 1910.

None of these buildings, not even the picturesque mock-Tudor toilets in the foreground, have survived, though the bus station continues on this site. What was not cleared away in development was lost when the whole station and most of its buses were blown up and burned during bombing in the Second World War.

On taking this view Fred Spalding tells us: 'The National Omnibus Company's first garage was in one of the railways arches. In June 1918, the Company purchased the yard and premises belonging to Messrs Wells and Perry, timber merchants. In June 1930 the old buildings were demolished and the present covered-in garage was opened in July 1931...'

This scene was photographed by Peter Russell – a 'pram protest' against a bus service introduced to the streets of Moulsham Lodge housing estate in the 1950s. 'We shall not be moved!'

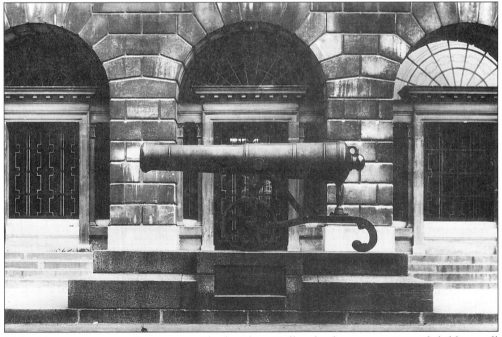

This old cannon cannot be seen outside the Shire Hall today but generations of children will remember it as the gun they climbed on at play in Oaklands Park. It is the barrel of a Russian gun, mounted on an unidentified, and rather inadequate carriage, presented to the town in 1858. It was moved to Oaklands in 1937.

An unusual view of Waterloo Lane looking towards New Street, with the old Police Station on the corner, as it appeared about 1935.

Now a department of the Anglia Polytechnic University, this building is seen just after its erection in 1962 to serve what was popularly known as the 'Chelmsford Tech'.

Four
Characters

Fred Spalding, the first, took this portrait around 1900 in his studio in Tindal Square. This little, old waggoner, name unknown, was remembered for his attitude to motor transport – 'Gimme 'osses, say I, an' 'ang they motor cars!'

Richard wears the official uniform and leans on the staff issued to him for his defence while patrolling the streets of Chelmsford through the night in the early-nineteenth century. Citizens, safe in the beds, would hear him regularly calling the hours as he passed by.

Richard Hasler, 'Dick the Pieman', who died in 1876, sold his hot pies in Tindal Square on market days. When his old wicker basket wore out his friends presented him with this up-to-date canister, engraved 'Hasler's Genuine No. 1.'

Corporal Thomas Bausor of the 4th Essex Volunteers. When he was not dressed up for training he kept the Red Cow Temperance Hotel in Broomfield Road, through the last years of the nineteenth century.

The painted scene at the back tells us that this is the first Spalding's studio in about 1864. Three men from Wells and Perry's brewery in Duke Street are portrayed in their working dress. Left to right: S. Hill in the short smock, T. Shonk in the long smock and Jos Isabel in a fustian jacket.

A wedding group of the 1890s, possibly at Stringfield Place; one of the Spalding family's rare omissions of full details.

Brig. Gen. Sir Evelyn Wood, VC, GC, GCMG (1838-1919), born at Cressing, came to the County Town on 14 October 1879 to receive, from the County of Essex...

...a Sword of Honour at the Shire Hall.

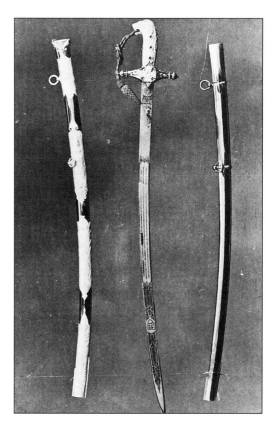

He can just be discerned standing at the front centre of the platform, in front of the middle door.

Mr Drake the Macebearer – the first man to walk before the Mayor on all official occasions carrying his highly decorated staff of office.

A composite picture gallery of all the members of the first ever Chelmsford Borough Council on 9 November 1888.

Fred Spalding's photograph of the original drawing for the Borough's coat of arms granted in 1888 as Chelmsford was officially incorporated as a Borough.

A hundred years ago the Judge's Carriage headed a solemn procession as the judge attended the first day of the Assize. The four horses seen in the 1762 print have now been reduced to two and by 1906 a car had been introduced and the glamour faded.

The last of the attendants on the Judge's carriage to the Assize in 1906.

In terms of people's work, wealth and happiness Guglielmo Marconi (1874-1937) probably had the greatest influence on Chelmsford of any individual in its history. Here he is seen operating his marvellous invention on board his yacht *Elettra* in around 1920.

The Marconi Wireless Works, specially built in 1912 as the firm outgrew its original premises in Hall Street. The aerials, still to be completed, rose to a height of 450 feet.

This picture is from a postcard in the Chelmsford Library's collection and bears the superscription, 'The first open motorbus in Essex, outside the White Hart (Chelmsford) *c.* 1910'. Thomas Clarkson pioneered this first steam bus and gave employment to hundreds of people in his Chelmsford factory.

There is an air of excitement about this group posing with the Clarkson steam-bus outside the Bell at Little Waltham.

Five

Houses

Highlands, or Hylands as we know it today, was built in 1728. It was extended with a grand portico, added between 1819 and 1825, which can be seen in this engraving of 1831.

A rear view of Hylands in 1964. The wings have now been reduced to one storey as they were originally constructed.

A view of Hylands from its park in 1978, before restoration by its owners, Chelmsford Borough Council.

The most important house in Chelmsford, until its demolition in 1808, was Moulsham Hall, the Manor House seat of the Mildmay family, landlords over a wide area around Chelmsford. Its earlier importance is now marked in the name of a modern housing estate – Moulsham Lodge.

Bishop's Hall was used as a sort of weekend residence for the Bishops of London down to the sixteenth century. It survived, although much restored and altered, until 1928, when it was demolished, as part of the Hoffmann works at the corner of Rectory Lane and New Street.

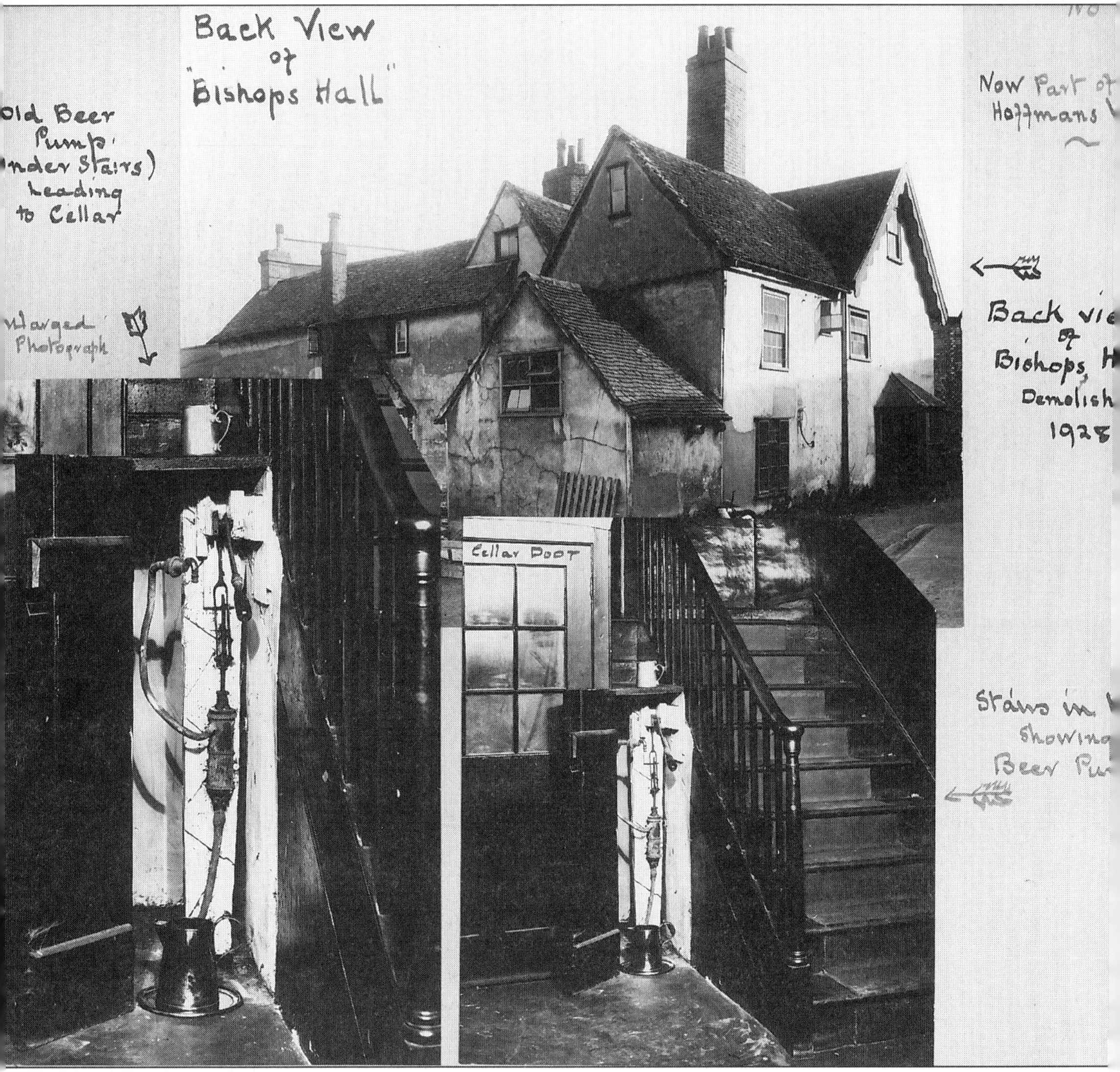
Back View
of
"Bishops Hall"
Old Beer
Pump
nder Stairs)
Leading
to Cellar
nlarged
Photograph
Now Part of
Hoffmans
Back vie
of
Bishops, H
Demolish
1928
Cellar Door
Stairs in
showing
Beer Pu

Fred Spalding made this photomontage to show Bishop's Hall from the rear and the interesting old beer pump.

How the other half lived: terraced houses for middle class people in Fairfield Road, where today the bus station, the Civic centre and its car park have been extended.

Chelmsford's only high-rise block of flats, erected by the Council in 1962 on the Melbourne estate.

Since 1945 housing estates have taken over acres of farmland to meet the demand for homes for workers in the booming electrical industries, radio, radar, television and mechanical engineering, not to mention shops and county and local government. Here the Chignal estate, complete in the 'sixties, shows a genuine attempt by planners to make Chelmsford a pleasant place to live.

Six
River Views

The date on the keystone proclaims the age of the Stone Bridge which took the increasing weight of modern traffic until recent pedestrianisation. The Meadows shopping mall now occupies the river bank on the lefthand side beyond the bridge.

WATERHOUSE LANE, CHELMSFORD,
Looking towards Rainsford Road.

Showing the old Wooden Bridge over the River "Can"
(View from a painting about 1874).

The New Bridge and Roadway was opened in 1922.
The old Windmill stood on the site now known as Mill House.

History has gone full circle in this scene to the extent that every feature, natural or architectural, has been removed. Spalding explains why, but since his day bridge and road have been altered again out of all recognition. Only the river runs on.

94

Here is the second chapter in the story of that bridge – a new bridge of iron has replaced the timber construction.

A view at the turn of the century, downstream, of the Stone Bridge over the Can. We are standing on the Iron Bridge, or New Bridge. Today we would see the length of Marks and Spencer's store along the left bank.

The old Springfield, or Bradridge's Mill and the miller's house in Victoria Road on a dismal day in 1975. This was the birthplace of Joseph Strutt, 1749-1802, celebrated artist and author of great works like *The Sports and Pastimes of the People of England.*

The old drainage pond formed when building the viaduct was year by year improved to the serenity of a lake and island refuge for wildlife, seen here on an April day in 1986.

This photograph of 1986 shows some of the extensive redevelopment of New London Road and the sympathetic restoration of a corner between the ring road and the river where thousands of crocuses light up a dull spring day.

The viaduct which takes the railway over the Chelmer, the division between the parishes of Springfield and Broomfield. The old, rough pastures have been sown and mown to lawn-like smoothness, making a pleasant approach to the town for pedestrians and cyclists.

MEADOW SIDE , SPRINGFIELD . 848 .

The Chelmer winds its way through the Springfield side of Chelmsford early this century. The houses stand in Meadowside, now Riverside. A footpath now runs along the bank in front of them.

The view upstream from the same point shows how close the houses have been built to the river by April 1986.

Seven

Inns

The lady in the crinoline shows that this was drawn well over a hundred years ago. At that time the Black Boy was an important coaching stop on the road from London to Norwich when the high road we now call the A12, left the town on this very corner where Springfield Road used to join the High Street. Now that junction is pedestrianised.

The Half Moon as it appeared in 1870. By 1930 the pressure of population and the increase in traffic it engendered were threatening the High Street and its old way of life.

The Half Moon in the great snowstorm of 1881. On Tuesday, 18 January it snowed for eleven hours from 10 a.m. and the drifts remained, following six weeks of frost, until well into April.

This painting of 1906 shows the Half Moon to be still very much in business.

The Cooper's Arms and the Swan Inn vie for custom in that part of Moulsham Street where Parkway runs today.

The Coach and Horses, built in 1870, and seen just before demolition in 1930. It adjoined the site of the old grammar school.

The Admiral Rous was built originally as a grandstand overlooking the Chelmsford Racecourse on Galleywood Common for the famous sporting Admiral. In this public house Samuel Crozier, landlord, killed his wife and became the last person to be hanged in Chelmsford prison.

A modern White Horse stands on this site, next to the parish church.

The Good Woman stood opposite the White Horse at Widford. Its sign had a headless woman on one side – so the local wits dubbed it the Silent Woman! On the other side was this portrait of Henry VIII, giving rise to the suggestion that it had at one time been called the King's Head. It has long since gone to dust.

The Red Cow had been a whole-hearted inn long before it became a Temperance Hotel as seen here in 1900, or thereabouts.

The Red Cow, on the corner of Broomfield Road and Duke Street, photographed at the same time. The tall lampposts were supplied with electricity by Crompton's, making it the first town in the whole of the country to have electric street lighting.

When old houses and businesses like the blacksmith's to the rear of the Angel Inn in Tindal Street were demolished in 1930, people thought it a shame to lose such historic places, but in the developments since 1960, all the buildings on this side of the street have now been demolished to make way for popular modern shopping precincts.

The dear old Spotted Dog, a popular pub particularly on market days, was another of Tindal Street's losses in the post-war purge. This is how its yard to the rear looked in 1937.

A further view of that same yard showing how, from the earliest times, craftsmen's workshops offered a wide variety of crafts and services to townspeople and visiting farmers.

Another of Spalding's valuable contributions to Chelmsford's history. When the old Golden Fleece was demolished in 1932, a copy of the *London Gazette* was found, published in 1699. In it was found an advertisement for the inn as 'a freehold and well repaired (it) hath convenient stables and outhouses, stands in the Market place (and) is to be sold at a reasonable rate.'

The Cross Keys on the Baddow Road side of the Stone Bridge, now pedestrianised, was replaced in 1916 by a completely new building, the Regent Theatre. It had been built in the fifteenth century and so was the last link Chelmsford had with its Medieval hostelries. But then, the theatre and the Bingo hall which followed have both closed down.

Chelmsford Brewery awaiting demolition in 1936. It was in Duke Street, almost on the corner of Victoria Road, where Dorset House was then the manager's house. All traces of it have been removed by road works and business buildings.

Eight

Churches

St Mary's, the parish church, before the clerestory was added over the east end in 1878. Right: The west doorway. The original is a good example of Spalding's method of mounting and annotation.

The church in 1850. The font shown is now in the museum. The Royal arms appear over the chancel arch and the galleries on either side were removed in 1873.

A tragedy – part of the church fell in on the night of 17 January 1800.

A view to the west of the ruins.

The masons at their work of restoration.

St Marys, Chelmsford

restored by Frederic Chancellor 1884 - £1400

Cleres added 187

Note Railing

Railing

The church rebuilt and as it looked at the beginning of the twentieth century. Note the photographer's comments.

Note
Chairs

Note
Gas
Standards

Banner-Stave L
or Cupboards
top ventilator
? Old Flags

The interior of the church then, again with the photographer's comments.

The parish church of St Mary before 1914 when it became a Cathedral.

The organ as recorded by Fred Spalding around 1930.

THE CATHEDRAL SPIRE.

For some considerable time past, the Cathedral Authorities have been somewhat apprehensive regarding the condition of the Cathedral spire, and more especially the lower framework. The main cause for anxiety has centred round the eight oak posts which carry the super-structure, and which, for at least half their total length, are entirely exposed to the weather. As the spire was erected a hundred and eighty-three years ago this exposure has naturally resulted in gradual deterioration and weakening of these particular timbers, more especially those on the south and west faces. The timbers in question are clearly visible to anyone standing at a convenient distance from the building, and appear just above the level of the top of the battlements. Another source of weakness was the framing supporting the main centre-post of the spire itself; this occurs at the base of the spire, immediately above the open space at the top of the broaching. In addition to the defective timbering it was also found that the lead covering of the spire had depreciated to a very serious extent, and wet was continually penetrating to the timbers and framework beneath. A further source of anxiety was the great weight of the lead—no less than three and a half tons—which the spire had to support. As the result of a recent examination and report by the Architect, the Rector and Wardens felt it imperative that this costly item of repair should be embarked upon without any further delay, the munificence of Mrs. Keene and her late husband having made the undertaking

possible. The services of Mr. Sharp (trading as Henry Potter), the well-known builder, were engaged, and a very ingenious piece of scaffolding was erected round the spire by his men.

The whole of the framework has now been carefully overhauled and greatly strengthened by the introduction of new timbers, and the structure put into a sound condition. In order to avoid the great weight of lead it was decided to cover the spire with copper, a far lighter and tougher material, and which is said to be even more durable than lead. In course of time and from exposure to weather copper turns an attractive shade of green, an example of which may be seen on the cupola surmounting the Drill Hall at the bottom of Market Road. The copper work has been carried out by the well-known firm of Messrs. F. Braby and Co., of Euston Road, and is a most interesting example of the copper smith's craft.

The repairs and gilding of the weather-vane were executed by the builder, and the lightning-conductor work by Messrs. Gray and Son, of High Holborn. The repairs are now nearing completion; most of the scaffolding has been removed, and the copper smiths are now at work on the flat round the base of the spire broaching. It may not be generally known that the weather-vane is wrought in copper, and represents a flying dragon, with open mouth and protruding tongue, and is a fine example of eighteenth century workmanship. It is, of course, entirely hand wrought, and the detail is exceptionally good; its total length is six feet six inches, while the ball immediately beneath is one foot ten inches in diameter.

The spire, of what is now the Cathedral, being restored in 1932. The eight oak timbers supporting it had been exposed to the weather for nearly two hundred years, and the weight of the old lead sheathing was replaced with lighter copper, giving it the green appearance we see today. The 6 ft 6 ins long weathervane is a flying dragon with open mouth and protruding tongue.

A view taken by Fred Spalding senior, in about 1870.

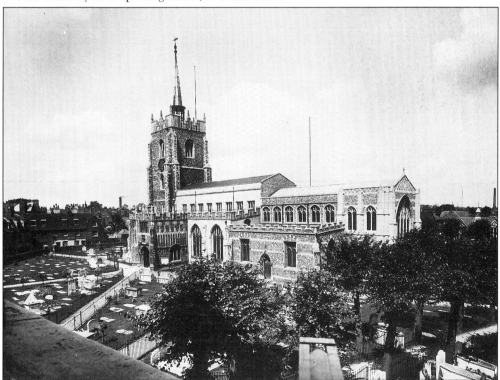

One of Spalding's postcards showing the addition of the clerestory at the east end.

The Cathedral, floodlit, in December 1932, celebrating completion of the restoration work.

The Mildmay monument, of 1557, in the cathedral with a Latin epitaph added by their son in 1571; it is to Thomas Mildmay, Lord of the manor of Chelmsford and Moulsham and Avice his wife. He with their eight sons and she with their seven daughters.

The Cathedral – the choir, the altar and the east window after the restoration.

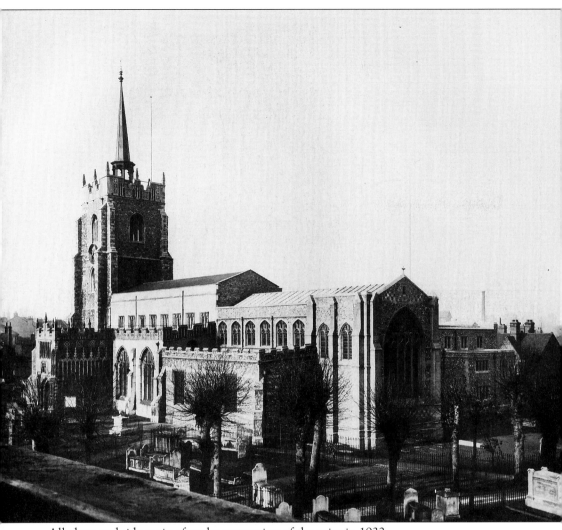

All clean and tidy again after the restoration of the spire in 1932.

The Chapel of the Holy Ghost at this time.

The Bishop, Sherard Falkner Allison DD, knocks on the Cathedral door at his enthronement as fourth Bishop of Chelmsford on 17 February 1951.

The Cathedral as it looked in 1978.

The Cathedral Close behind Duke Street and Tindal Square.

Restoration of St. John's Church, Moulsham.

Local workman proudly pose at the top of the tower of St John's church, Moulsham, as it undergoes restoration through the winter of 1932. Insert: The finished result seen in the following summer.

Nine

Shops

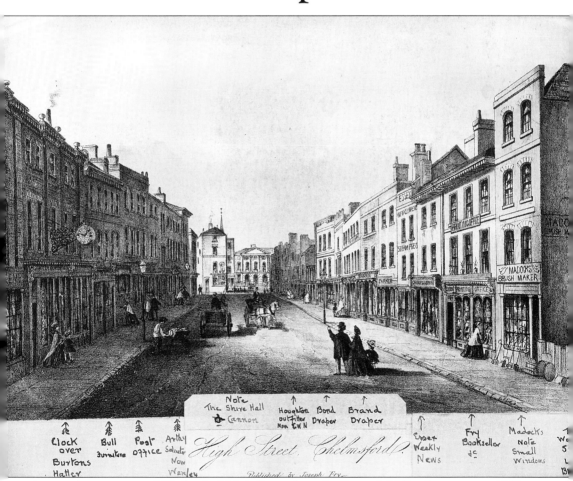

An artist's impression of Chelmsford High Street from the Springfield Road junction in 1863.
The original annotations are by Fred Spalding.

Old shops in Tindal Square, opposite the Shire Hall in about 1915. By 1921 they had gone to dust and the Midland Bank had risen on that site.

The strangely shaped frontage of the shop at 11 Duke Street is due to the fact the building was once a blacksmith's forge and horses were led in here off the street. The milk churn helps us to date it to the 1920s. The frontage was later straightened in a road-widening scheme and the houses on the right were demolished.

Spalding's classic picture of Tindal Square 120 years ago, showing his family's shop in the centre. The men sitting on the wagon shafts await their fellow farm labourers who are riding about the town collecting money from shops where the farmer dealt through the year, for their 'largesse' – tips with which to buy beer to celebrate the 'harvest home'.

The same scene taken by the younger Fred Spalding in the 1930s. The road is wholly paved, cars are king and every shop has changed hands since the earlier picture.

Bond's, now Debenham's, was Chelmsford's first department store and this is how it looked in the 1930s.

This corner development, where Moulsham Street met The Friars, replaced the old houses and the former Friary gateway in 1932. Within thirty years they were demolished because they lay in the path of the ring road, Parkway.